Zane Hogan
101 Hunting Jokes
© 2017, Zane Hogan
Self-published

zanehoganbooks@gmail.com

101

Hunting Jokes

By: Zane Hogan

A man and woman were on their first date. The woman was trying to make conversation and said, "So I hear you hunt deer." The man suddenly turned bright red.

"What's wrong?" asked the woman.

"I'm not used to someone calling me dear on the first date," the man said.

Why didn't the hunter want to shoot reindeer?

He didn't caribou't them.

What kind of rabbit did the hunter see through his scope?

A cross hare.

Why is it hard to hunt for boars in the summer?

Because they prefer not to be bacon in the heat.

I hate when suddenly a deer holds up a rifle

and gives me a taste of my own venison.

A hunter got on his hands and knees to get a better look at some tracks.

And that's how he got hit by the train.

What do bighorn sheep do when they get lost?

They bleat around the bush.

Why didn't the hunter want to eat pheasant?

He heard it was grouse.

Two hunters were driving through the country to go bear hunting.

They came upon a fork in the road where a sign said "BEAR LEFT" so they went home.

What should a sick hunter do?

Have a little coughy and get on with it.

What did the bear tracks give the hunter?

Paws for concern.

Why did the camp cook stir-fry the venison?

Because he liked to wok on the wild side.

A 10-point buck walked into a restaurant and ordered a burger and fries. The waitress said, "We don't see too many deer around here."

"At these prices," replied the buck, "I'm not surprised."

What happened when the hunter tried to shoot a moose with a BB gun?

He ended up in hunters' a pellet court.

I knew a woman who would start talking like a deer when she was stressed.

What a weird-doe.

Why should you be careful when cutting up a moose?

You could easily make a big moose steak.

What do you call a duck who hides in a henhouse during duck season?

Chicken.

How did the man buy food for his hunting dog?

By the pound.

What happened to the bighorn sheep hunter went he went the wrong way?

He made a ewe turn.

I can't think of the best kayak brand for a duck hunter,

canoe?

Hunters will often hang up their deer together

to make ends meat.

What did the cold hunter do when he got a flat tire?

He had to jacket up.

Why did the hunter stop making his own liquor?

It was too much of a whiskey business.

A deer hunter asked his pastor if it was a sin to hunt on Sunday.

"From what I hear about your aim," said the pastor, "It's a sin for you to hunt on any day."

What does Kermit the Frog hunt for?

Rabbit, rabbit.

Two hats were hanging on a set of antlers.

One hat says to the other, "You stay here, I'll go on a head."

Why do some hunters prefer bow hunting?

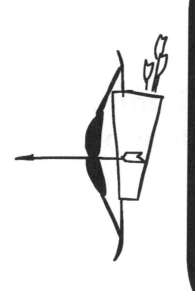

It's the only way they can get their point across.

What do you call a deer that uses his left and right hooves equally well?

Bambi-dextrous.

What kind of flooring do alligator hunters prefer?

Reptiles.

Why was the hunter flustered during his speech?

He had to keep rifle-ing through his notes.

What did the cold duck hunter realize when he started a fire in his boat?

You can't have your kayak and heat it too.

What's a hunter's favorite cereal?

Bucky Charms.

What happened when the camp cook ran out of duck seasoning?

He just winged it.

If hunters don't argue what they do?

De-bait.

What did the buck tell his son to do as soon as he grew horns?

Go to Venice, son.

What happened when the hunter went to buy a camouflaged shirt?

He couldn't find one.

I shot my first turkey today.

It scared the heck out of everyone in the frozen food section.

What do you get when you cross Bambi with a ghost?

Bamboo.

I notice that all ducks close their eyes when hiding from hunters.

Except one, the Peking duck.

How did the wet hunter buy a poncho in the rain forest?

With his Amazon gift card.

Why did the cold hunter lay down next to the woodstove?

He wanted to sleep like a log.

Why did the hunter stop shooting birds in December?

He decided to quit cold turkey.

What happened when the hunter got lost in the mist?

He didn't have the foggiest idea where he was.

Who always roots
for the Bucks
even when
they're losing?

The
Deerleaders.

For meat, some hunters eat sheep

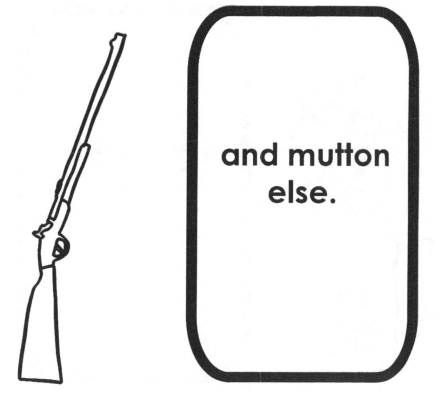

and mutton else.

Remember
never go hunting
with a bat.

It will keep
flying away.

Who is the best at operating a shotgun?

A doctor.

What does Matt Damon do when he needs camouflage pants?

He goes Goodwill hunting.

What's the difference between a hunter and a fisherman?

A hunter lies in wait.

A fisherman waits and lies.

Why was the
bighorn sheep
cold?

He lost his
muttons.

How can you clone deer?

Buy a doe-it-yourself kit.

What do you call a guy with a recently shot duck?

A dead winger for Hunter.

Once salt was invented

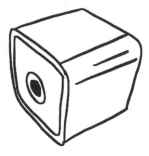

the hunter's problem was licked.

Why couldn't the buck parallel park?

He didn't have a deerview mirror.

What do you call your hunting buddy when he accidentally shoots himself in the rear?

A real pain in the butt.

Why is the bearded hunter never hungry?

He mustache his food in there.

Did you hear about the deer population?

It's staggering.

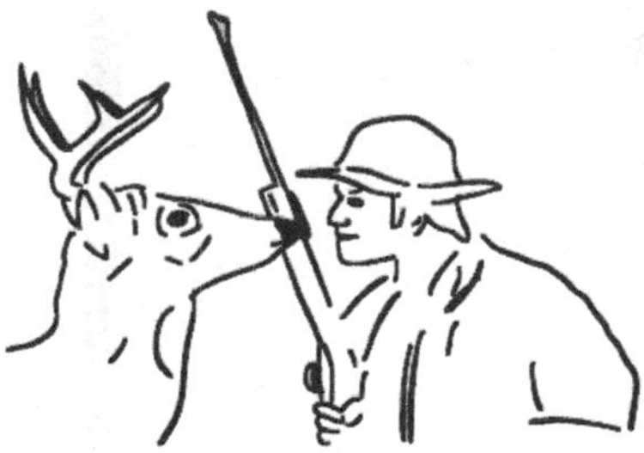

What happened
when the
longhorn sheep
saw the hunter?

He became
a little ram-
bunctious.

What happened to the hunter when he lost his bottle of gin?

He became very dis-spirited.

Why didn't the hunter like the bear stew?

It was a little grizzly.

What's the best thing to have when hunting?

A game plan.

Did one hunter blame the other for not shooting the deer?

No, because they don't pass the buck.

What is the best way to hunt bear?

With your clothes off.

What do you call
a hunter who
brags about the
size of his bullets?

A real big
shot.

The wolf hunter
tried to sing

but he
didn't know
howl.

Did you hear about the explosion at the deer packing plant?

It was quite the meatier shower.

Why did the
hunter get
squeamish when
he was dressing
the deer?

It was a gut
reaction.

A hunter leapt over his rifle when he heard the chipmunk.

That's what you call jumping the gun.

Why did the hunter keep missing his target?

He didn't aim deerectly for it.

Did you hear about the pig hunter who told long stories?

He was a total boar.

What do bowhunters study in school?

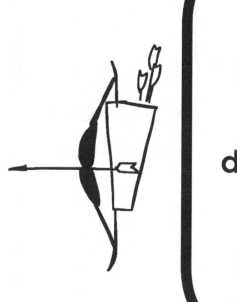

Arrow dynamics.

What do you get if you cross a telephone with a hunting dog?

A golden receiver!

I've never actually killed a deer before,

but I'd like to take a shot at it.

Why did the hunter use photographs for target practice?

He wanted some snap shots.

What does a poet need before he goes hunting?

A poetic license.

Spoiled deer meat

is a dead loss.

A man is out hunting and kills a deer. He brings it home to his family and cooks it, but doesn't tell his kids what it is. He said "I'll give you a hint, it's what your mother calls me."

The youngest son cries out, "It's bird brain, don't eat it!"

If hunters don't argue what they do?

De-bait.

What is the best tip for hunting?

Sorry there are no easy antlers.

What did the
moose take for
indigestion?

An
elkaseltzer.

I was hoping to get promoted at the Buckskin Slipper Company,

but I could never get my foot in the deer.

What is a duck hunter's favorite game to play?

Billiards.

Why was the hunter confused in in forest?

He couldn't cedar wood for the trees.

What did the hunter say when he took a sip of cold coffee?

Cool beans.

What do you a call a hunter who's cold, lost and can't locate camp?

Ice-olated.

Smells at hunting camp

are noted
according
to rank.

I was going to tell you I saw a 20-point buck lying in his bed,

but I made it up.

When does a hunter eat raw venison?

Only on rare occasions.

What do you call an exhausted rifle?

A shot gun.

The hunters found the dead deer with exit wounds but no entry wounds.

It was obviously an inside job.

Why was the drunk hunter happy?

Because he was in high spirits.

The hunter wondered why the tree branch was getting bigger.

Then it hit him.

Made in the USA
Monee, IL
03 October 2022

15178958R10059